Wild Edric

'They come upon me like an evening cloud,
Stranger than moon-rise, whiter than a shroud.
They are as secret as the black cloud-shadows
Sliding along the ripe midsummer grass;
With a breath-taking majesty they pass.'

Mary Webb: *Presences*

 WILD EDRIC

A Narrative Poem

Nigel Sustins

MARCHLAND BOOKS 2008

Published by
Marchland Books
Rose Cottage, Wentnor
Bishops Castle
Shropshire SY9 5EE

ISBN 978-0-9558589-0-1

Designed and typeset in Ehrhardt
(with ornaments by William Morris)
at Five Seasons Press, Hereford
and printed by Biddles Ltd, Norfolk, UK

CONTENTS

Prologue: The Cave

The stone is sealed, the darkness dribbles down like a miasma at the
Back of vision. He places his fingers on the rock, massages it as though
Seeking a secret lever that might spring open to release him. The
Imprisonment in earth seems both recent and age-old, the wounds
From the final battle still raw, yet the blood long dried and blackened.
He breathes on the rough surface, to prove that he is alive, but
The movement of air may be centuries of spiders' webs dropping
Into infinity. Certainly, his companions no longer breathe. He has
Felt his way from one to the other, and they are quiet and cold.
He is the last. Yet the passion for life does not abate. His mouth forms
A word: 'Godda'; not a prayer, but an invocation to the woman he
Has loved and lost.

When it was clear that the battle was wrested from him, Edric took his sword,
Thrust it into its sheath, and whistled for Gethrin his hound. The dog came
At great speed, and to his jaws Edric committed the blade. Gethrin raced away,
Knowing the hiding place.

So the means of overturning still abides, if only he can reach through the
Rock and snatch the days to come from a horde of impossibilities.

Book One: The Finding of Godda

When the sea savaged the land, and all the rivers on that shore
Turned tail, flooding back into the heart of Britain, the cliffs
Crumbled, and the beaches were scattered with shells like the
Tiny skulls of men. A new King ascended, his hose barely wet,
Surveying the acres of water with a stony stare.

Edric was not there to meet him. His sway was over lands far
From the eroded coast: in Shropshire, and on the borders where
Wales gnawed its English neighbours with teeth whetted on
Bloody fields. Edric looked from Pole Tower high on the
Myndd, towards the Stippled Stones, feeling a movement deep
Within the earth. It was hardly a tremble, the faintest echo of
Ancient quakes in which few would now believe, even on viewing
The patterns riven in the granite, and the barren cone of Clee rising
Like a frozen wave. It was not even a scent on the breeze, although
Gethrin the hound wrinkled his nose, before being quickly distracted
By a passing bee, and Gwentor the horse whinnied nervously,
Rolling her eyes across the empty moor.

In the months that came after, Edric could sense a constraint like
Chains falling slowly from the skies, destined to weight a yoke
Around his neck. He beckoned to his allies, Bleddyn and Rywall,
Welsh princes whose fortunes were so closely intertwined with

Edric's, that they formed part of his retinue: bold, dark-haired
Brothers with the eyes of vigilant hawks. 'Set men to ride the circuit
Of our lands, keeping watch on who comes and goes. Let them report
Any strangers. And now, I think a hunt is stirring. We must take
Horse and hound before we ourselves fall prey to predators.'

Many a time did Edric ride with his companions, and a pack of
Black hounds, to hunt. They roamed from Hopesay to Clun,
Galloped across Rhadley Hill, and the spine of the Stippled Stones,
Driving deer and boar from cover. The hounds worked well,
Fearsome and slaver-flecked as they bayed. And Gethrin,
Though brindled-brown, ran close to his master's horse,
The fine-stepping silver-thewed Gwentor, and the pack did
Not deny him.

News came of a stranger, riding covertly in the hills. Bleddyn
And Rywall tracked him down to a waterfall on the Myndd: a
Lithe man dressed all in leather, with a bow and quiver to hand.
Soon his arms were pinioned by the Welsh pair, and they thrust
His head under the gushing stream. He came up scattering droplets
And oaths. Trussed like a deer, he was slung across his own
Horse's saddle. 'Your words are few,' said Bleddyn, laughing.
'But we will let our Master Edric hear them. And he will decide
Whether or not to cut them short.'

The stranger would not give his name, so Rywall dubbed him:
'Leathershanks'. Now he stood, bound, outside the Lords' hall

At Lydbury. Edric came forth, his tangled thicket of hair flying
From his shoulders, his beard brown and copious, his nose buzzard-
Beaked, his eyes ever restless, roaming the contours of his land,
And then settling with sudden concentration on Leathershanks.
Edric tapped the hilt of his sword. 'Enemies of our domain have a
Right: to better acquaintance with my sword. By what wisdom may
You be spared?' Leathershanks thought long, beads of sweat
Breaking on his brow. He gazed at the men assembled, more
Gathering every moment, from garth and stable, warriors of
Edric's fealty. 'You may do with me what you will,' he said sullenly,
'But my kinsman has turned his eyes on these lands, and will not
Leave me unavenged.' Edric seated himself on a trestle in the yard,
And folded his arms. 'Tell us of this kinsman of yours. Why should
He be concerned with our peaceful shire?' Leathershanks moistened
His tongue, preparing his tale. 'He has at his back the might of the
New French King: mail, sword and horse. But he is also a prince
In his own right: from the West, where rebellion is quick to flare,
And many follow him to seek their due. The French are busy, to
North and South, building their castles, biding their time. My kinsman
Steps in the breach, looks for land to claim, so that when the Normans
Begin their quest for new domains, he will be there already,
Firmly established and alert.' Edric savoured these ambiguous words.
'So this kinsman: is he saviour or supplanter?' 'He rides his own course,
Bowing to no man.' 'And yet he has the might of France at his back,'
Said Edric, softly revealing the prisoner's guile.

Bleddyn beckoned Edric aside, out of earshot. 'I think I know of this
Man: Drænog the Shunned, a renegade Welsh prince, so hedged about
That no-one knows his face. He gathers to himself wastrels and fortune-
Hunters, wine-soused brigands, now no doubt augmented by French
Soldiers who think he holds the key to subduing the borderlands.'
Edric drank in these words, and returned to questioning his prisoner.
'You would have us believe your kinsman is come to strengthen us,
Build a bulwark against the Norman tide. But is it not the truth that
He will quell us, and then betray us into the French King's hands?
Tell him we are well-defended here. We do not submit to foreign
Warlords, or Welsh invaders. Go back and deliver our message:
Keep from these hills!'

Edric drew a knife, and swiftly approached the prisoner. He cut
The man's bonds, and threw them aside. He signalled to the
Liege-man who held the captured horse, and Leathershanks was
Given leave to go, stripped of his weapons. There was a gasp of
Astonishment from those close by, but the Lord simply waved
A long finger dismissively. Leathershanks struggled into the saddle,
And jerked his bridle roughly, impatient to be gone. As he left
The yard, Edric pointed the raised finger at two horsemen, who
Wheeled their mounts and set out to follow.

The companions of the hunt drew near, Bleddyn and Rywall
Blustering, unable to believe that Edric had let an enemy go
Unscathed. Ælfric, stout and ruddy of face, clamped his teeth
Together as though refusing rotten meat. Young Erwine, ever

Carefree, looked from one to the other, and simply smiled.
Dafydd the joker approached, long-limbed, pot-bellied, his arms
Swirling as though about to wrest a marvel from the air.

'My Lord!,' he said. 'You see that your brethren are perturbed.
They think this Leathershanks will go straight back to his camp,
Declaring how weak we are, how ready to fall.' Dafydd made a
Sucking noise, as though savouring his brew (of which he was
Over-fond). 'But it could be otherwise. Mercy does not
Betoken weakness. It is the enemy who is weak and foolish if he
Thinks he can outwit a man of Edric's stature.' Erwine cheered,
Ælfric spluttered. The two Welsh brothers marched forward
Until they were face to face with their Lord. Edric, two inches
Taller, looked at them both. 'Say what you will.' Bleddyn glanced
Downwards as though seeking inspiration from the dust, but
Said nothing. Rywall spat on the ground. 'Bleddyn has not yet
Had enough ale to convince you of this folly. Drænog is a wolf
Running unchecked amongst the sheepfolds.' Edric clapped the
Two princes on the shoulder. 'Leathershanks is followed. When
Our men return, we will know more about his kinsman and the lair
In which he lurks. Meanwhile, let no one despair. We still have time
And courage, and do not lightly put our lands at risk. We will wait
And learn, plan and prepare. No wolf shall harry our flock until we
Have an arrow aimed at its mangy hide.'

The two riders kept Leathershanks in sight all through the long
Afternoon. The man led them a circuitous dance across the Myndd,

Always visible, as though saying: 'I am not in haste; you will tire
Before I do.' Just as dusk was gathering, Leathershanks rode
For the Stippled Stones, spurring on his horse, not looking
Back. He cantered up the slope towards the looming shadows
Of the Devil's Throne, and here he paused, glanced over his
Shoulder, and waved at his pursuers. Then he was amongst
The stones, hooves clattering eerily. Edric's men rode hard,
But when they came to the Throne, there was no sign of their
Mark. The wind whistled in the decaying teeth of the rocks.
Darkness fell. They were marooned without sight or sense.

Next day saw Edric and his band of five at this same spot,
Keeping to the cover of the stones in case a long-distance
Arrow should find them. A track went down the slope on
The other side, grass bruised where horse's hooves had trod.
The hills to the west were hazy: there was no clear sign of
Settlement or camp. And yet it was in Edric's mind that
Leathershanks had not had far to go, unless he could see
In the dark. They took the track, which soon descended
Into a green-guarded gully that hid both horse and man.
Forest surged forward to meet them, a haven for boar and
Deer that Edric had raided on occasion. But now they hunted
Only the signs of recent passage, Gethrin primed by a good
Whiff of the weapons that Leathershanks had left behind.

They came to a clearing that none of them knew, well-hidden
In the forest. A wooden dwelling stood at the centre, dappled

By the shadows of leaves. Gethrin's low growl showed that
Leathershanks had paused here, gazing perhaps on the
Mysterious house as they did now, or making for a spot
Already known to him. Edric felt a prickling of the skin,
Presage of danger. The house had signs of habitation: a
Large pile of chopped logs outside the door, horses tethered
To the rail of a long gallery. The six watched, Erwine with
An arrow ready-notched. The door opened, and a stocky
Man rolled forth, red-faced, clad in a garment made from
The hide of bear or wolf. He glanced around the clearing,
Sauntering to the horses, stroking them. As he did so, with
His back to the watchers, his voice rang clear: 'You may as
Well show yourselves, or we shall thrust and parry in
Indecision until doomsday'. Edric and his companions
Stepped forward, parting the bushes. The man turned,
Giving them an appraising stare. 'Ah, not the ones who
Have lurked there before.' He came to meet them, and
Edric noticed the sword swinging from his hip. 'The tallest
Of you I know by reputation,' he said, smiling grimly.
'Edric of Shropshire is it not? Called "the Wild" for his
Knowledge of the woodland beasts, and a share of their cunning.
I am Oastwald, a simple woodsman, living here for many
A year, and thriving on the gifts of soil and forest.' He stopped
At ten paces from his new arrivals, arms folded and feet
Planted firmly on the ground.

Edric turned his gaze to five more figures suddenly emerging
From the house, women dressed in leather riding-suits,
Four of them tall and graceful, the fifth shorter, darker in
Complexion, and wearing a headpiece with a curved nose-guard
Like an owl's beak, partially hiding her features. 'My daughters,' said
Oastwald, 'and . . . a guest.' All noise was hushed in the glade:
No bird or insect intruded. The thrumming that Edric felt was like
The deep movement of blood in his veins as he looked at the fifth
Woman, and she raised her eyes to his.

'You speak true. I am Edric, and these my close companions.
We follow the trail of a man caught spying, agent of a renegade
In league with the King of France.' Oastwald snorted. 'Kings mean
Little to me. I am disposed to think better of those who leave me
In peace. The spy you speak of must be the one who has skulked
Nearby. I think he has envy towards us, or lust for my daughters.'
At these words, the women shifted restlessly. 'We mean you no
Harm', assured Edric. And his eyes were drawn again to the smallest
Of the five, and he saw that however much she tried to hide her face,
Her beauty was apparent.

'Come!' said Oastwald, extending his arms, 'you are welcome here.
We have food prepared. Bring your horses: tether them at the rail.'
Edric and his companions stepped back to fetch their mounts, and
Oastwald led the way towards the house. Just as the horses were
Tied, Gethrin—still amongst the trees—gave a sharp bark, and when
Edric wheeled, there was no sign of him. Instead, a familiar figure

Appeared from the fringes of the wood, his tanned features wrinkling
In humour. Edric put his hand to his sword, but Leathershanks raised a
Hand in warning. 'You are covered by marksmen who could pierce
Your eye with an arrow before your blade is lifted. Now, walk towards
The centre of the glade, unstrapping your weapons. Place them in a
Heap—there!' An arrow ripped across the clearing, striking the ground
With a vibrant thud. Edric's eyes darted to his companions, and one
By one they gave an almost imperceptible nod. They walked slowly towards
The quivering arrow, unbuckling their belts, and threw down their swords
And bows with a clash of metal. Leathershanks smiled approvingly.
'And now you, woodsman, do the same.' Oastwald frowned, but
Obeyed. 'And whilst you are there, let us see your woodmanship.
Bring logs, and make a healthy stack close by the weaponry.'
Oastwald busied himself. He glanced at Edric, and both knew the
Reason: fire would consume house and weapons. When the logs
Were high, Oastwald cast a questioning look at Leathershanks, but
He knew the answer. He brought a flint from his coat, and struck a
Flame, holding it to the dry woody sprigs at the bottom of the pile.
The fire grew, yellow and orange, flickering in the glade. Leathershanks
Moved position, so he had everyone in view. 'I have watched this
House on many occasions, and often thought how good it would be
To see these damsels dance. One last entertainment.'

He waved his hand towards the women. 'Often, you must have enlivened
The evenings with dance and song. Come, show us how those long limbs
Move.' The five women took but a moment to collect themselves, and
Stepped forward in front of the fire, turning gracefully as Leathershanks

Devoured their suppleness. Dafydd made an unexpected, but carefully
Considered move. Holding his arms out wide, and twirling his hands,
He moved nonchalantly towards the nearest of the sisters, and joined
Her in a solemn round. Bleddyn, Rywall and Erwine too sauntered
Towards the dance floor, bowing to the other sisters. Leathershanks
Was at first suspicious, but then raised his hand to stall the archers,
And folded his arms to watch the courtliness which would precede
Death. Edric came last, inclining towards Oastwald's 'guest', whilst
Ælfric, not fond of dancing, contented himself with clapping a
Beat. The dancers moved close, but did not touch, and Edric
Felt the breath of the woman he partnered upon his neck. Her
Eyes flicked upwards, and as the other pairs swirled in front of
Leathershanks' sight, she drew without stooping, a long blade
From her leather boot, pushing it towards Edric. He stiffened
For a moment, but then thrust it back at her, mouthing: 'It is
Yours to use as you will.'

A high call, a trilling sound like that of a bird deep in the forest,
Pierced the air. The flames of the fire crackled, and smoke drifted
Across the clearing. A dog's bark echoed as if from all quarters,
Travelling as a wheel spins, followed by the cries of men nipped
At the heel. Gwentor neighed, heeding her master's surreptitious
Cry, pulled at her tether, broke loose and charged towards the
Fire, hooves dislodging the topmost brands as she leapt. In the
Confusion of smoke and scattered sparks, Edric and his men
Ran, crouching low, towards their weapons. The woman with
The blade threw it spinning in the air, cutting off Leathershanks'

Thumb as he raised his hand to ward off the threat. Men stumbled
From their hiding places, Gethrin, as fleet as a whirlwind pack
Of hounds, snapping at them from behind. Erwine and Ælfric
Launched their arrows, Bleddyn and Rywall hacked at the
Floundering forms. Oastwald reached to the base of the fire,
Drew forth a concealed axe which he wielded with relish. One
Attacker still stood, bemused, and as Edric ran to close with
Him, a creature of fur and fang dropped from the trees, long-
Bodied, sleek, sinking its teeth into the enemy's neck.

Leathershanks alone survived amongst the foe, his blood seeping
Into the ground. The woman who had felled him stood guard,
And as the glade filled with activity - the sisters calming the horses,
Oastwald and Dafydd dousing the fire, the other companions
Scouring the woods for further peril—Edric approached her.
'Lady, may I know your name?' 'I am Godda, under the protection
Of my woodsman host.' Bleddyn and Rywall came up behind,
Gazing down at the wounded captive. 'Time now perhaps for
The treatment he should have received at first?' said Bleddyn.
'Lady Godda gave the blow,' replied Edric. 'His fate shall be
Her decision.' Godda looked round at the impatient Welshmen,
But was not coerced. 'His wound can be salved, his horse retrieved.
Let him ride back with a message no one can doubt.' Edric nodded,
And turning to the Welsh pair said: 'But this time bind him across
The saddle, muffle his tongue, and let his horse lead you to the
Enemy's camp.'

When Bleddyn and Rywall had ridden out with Leathershanks,
Edric looked for a sign of the furred creature from the trees,
And found only Gethrin sniffing at the place it had last appeared.
'My Lady Godda, this fierce animal who has fought with us
Today: has it an affinity with you?' Godda smiled. 'He is in
My company, but a wild beast still.' 'And what is he called?'
'The Daleath: last of his kind, as I too am the last of my line.'

Interlude

He sits like an ancient king on a carved wooden throne.
Below him, human life seethes and putrefies, a pot of offal,
With scum spilling over the rim. He is known derisively as
'Drænog'. That suits him well, for the hedge-pig after
Which he is named, puts up its spikes to keep enemies at bay.
His true identity is shielded from all except a trusted few.
His army is called a rabble, his intentions maligned, but there
Is a carefully veiled strategy beneath the appearance of disarray.
The fact that Shalkin has been followed to the camp is of little
Consequence, since soon the troops will leave as winter draws on.
The Shropshire Lord can rest easy awhile. But his callous injury
To Shalkin, the only man whom Drænog loves, will not be
Forgotten. The severed thumb that rots on Edric's land will
Grow into a canker to blight his heart's desire.

Book Two: The Shield of Cawr

Winter sealed the borderlands, quietening the tread of distant armies,
Freezing for a while the incoming flood. Snow blanketed the Myndd,
Made passage difficult for horse and traveller. Seclusion
Brought confidence that enemy eyes would not roam far. A white
Peacefulness settled on home and garth for a season of respite.

Edric housed the rescued Oastwald and his clan in Wentnor lodge
Close to the Myndd. In return for a secure haven, Oastwald made
His borrowed home a place of hospitality, entertaining the Lord
And his men, his daughters providing food and ale: four women,
Close in age, whose mother had died in the forest on a day of
Tempestuous gales. Young men would ride by the house to catch
A glimpse of the fair sisters: Cwen, Gayna, Linn and Mae, and
Stayed for merriment and dance. Oastwald played the lyre, and
Godda—keeping somewhat aloof—the harp. So Edric came
From time to time, not for the dance, but engrossed by Godda's
Music. Her face, although half-hidden by black lustrous hair,
Was his true point of meditation, but he took only the occasional
Glance, and then fed on the memory as the harp plucked his
Senses: eyes of bright crystal, the cheekbones high, skin
Translucent with the glow of dark coral.

Invisible as the seeds and tubers beneath the snow, the
Gestation of Edric's love carried into the spring. When
The first wayside flowers began to bloom, he asked himself:

'How can a man of my age, who has already seen one wife
To the grave, set his heart on so youthful a form?'

One morning they rode together to Pole Tower, so that Edric
Could show Godda all his lands spread out below, shadows
Chasing across the sunlit fields as though blown by the
Wind. 'My lady, you are wise enough to read my intentions.
I am an old man, grizzled and ill-mannered. I know how
Precious to me are the lands in which I was reared. I know
Too that since I first looked upon you, there is someone
As precious as my heritage.' Godda smiled, and took his arm,
A warm sensation tingling in his flesh. 'Lord Edric, you
Demean yourself. You are yet in your prime, a man of honesty
And compassion.' Edric shook his head. 'It has not always been so.

They call me "the Wild", for in my younger days I was headstrong
And foolish, quick to taint my fingers with the blood of beast
And man.' 'My fingers too are not without stain,' said Godda
Quietly. 'My Lady, the future is uncertain. These lands now
So peaceful, may soon be witness to war and destruction.
Can there be a way for both of us to enjoy the pleasure
That remains?' She pressed his arm, but said nothing.
Edric looked closely in her eyes. 'Will you be my wife?'
In the fields below a curlew gurgled its cry, like bubbles rising
From the bed of a stream to break in the open air. 'Should I
Ask leave of your father? Where is he to be found?' A small
Grimace passed over Godda's face. 'If I am to marry you,

Promise that you will not seek out my origin, or question
Those who know me. I need no father's permission to wed.
Here: I give my answer as yes, if you are true to your pledge.'

Edric's heart was light at these words, for why should he want
To learn of her origin, when it was her presence now that
Delighted him? 'I make that promise, my Lady.' She looked
At him with the shadow of a storm-cloud on her brow.
'Know that if you break your word, our life together will be
Severed, the road I follow away from your hearth.' 'Heaven
Forbid that I should ever cause such injury!' declared Edric
With firm assent, and he bent his head to kiss her.

As spring budded, Godda and Edric were married with great
Pomp and ceremony. Oastwald's smile spread, and his four
Daughters were the bride's honorary sisters, garlanded with
Flowers. All Edric's people shared the long hours of feasting
And celebration. And so keen was Edric to extract the utmost
Joy from this event, he put aside suspicion that not all
The wedding guests were of his fiefdom, and only later
Did he think again of certain cloaked figures who rode their
Horses slowly out of Lydbury. But Bleddyn and Rywall had
Seen them, and followed as far as the Stippled Stones, where
They melted into the distant woodland. The encampment at
Shelve was shown to them, when Leathershanks' horse
Had carried its human burden there unerringly. Now perhaps
It was occupied again.

Night drew on, and Edric led his wife to a bridal bed beneath
Flower-decked canopies on the great lawn. After the passion
Of love-making, blissful sleep. Edric woke before dawn to
Hear strange cries echoing in the wood. The Daleath had made
Himself the guardian of their bower. The cries ceased, and
Edric had a sudden presentiment that his bride was not beside
Him. He put out his hand, expecting a cold vacant place. But
Godda was there, her body warm, her breathing gentle, like
The brushing of a midnight moth on the canvas of the tent.

The early days of love were unclouded and sweet. Edric thanked
The gods, for he had not succumbed to the Christ religion, but
Favoured the old deities, battle-hardened warriors who dwelt
In northern lands, bleak and weary, still clinging to their valour.
News came of travellers in the western shire, peddlers and story-
Spinners, not openly aggressive but weaning to their wares the
Country dwellers with their superstitious ways. Rumours grew of
Danger, not from an invading army, but from more insidious foes:
An underworld of demons that made their presence felt in the
Evening mists, and the cold, stony silence of the hills. The centre
Of the peril was the Devil's Throne, where—it was said—the
Demons gathered, and plotted mischief. Edric tried to counter
These idle fears, but perturbation spread, like streams from
Rain-soaked moors, pooling in muddied minds.

A day of storm pelted the hills, rain falling hard enough to
Prick the skin, jagged lightning in the sky, and a clatter of
Thunder rolling over the Myndd. Eyes turned towards the
Stippled Stones, awaiting the omen that had been foretold.
That night, in the rays of a full moon, Edric and Godda with
The five trusted companions, watched from Pole Tower.
A soft sheen garnished the hides of sheep and cattle in the
Pasture lands. Distant drumming stirred the hills, like
The memory of thunder, echoing and insistent. Lights
Flickered on the Stippled Stones, the torches—so it would
Be believed—of creatures from the nether world massing
For their rite. The moon was tawny as old gold above their
Heads, and the trees swayed in a dark ancient dance. A
White owl swooped in the fields below, but Edric felt no
Fear more than the brief mouse-tremor in the long grasses.

A great orange ball grew above the Devil's Throne, like
The morning sun about to break over the ranges. It crested
The jagged teeth of the stones, rocked to and fro with spitting
Flame, and crashed upon the rocks below, shattering into
Blazing fragments. The cry of those who watched throughout
Edric's land seemed to gather in a gigantic sigh, and a distant
Ripple of thunder rolled around the hills. Edric turned to his
Wife and companions: 'Here is a marvel indeed! Shall we ride
To inspect it at first hand?' All those close by said: 'Aye!',
And they stepped down from the tower to find their horses
Spirited but biddable.

Towards the west they rode, under the racing moon, Edric
Astride Gwentor, Godda on her white mare, all seven
Spurring forwards. The silence of the countryside rushed
To engulf them, but they sliced through the night, a hunt
Without hounds, save Gethrin, letting their wild cries carry
To the foot of the Stippled Stones, and the strange smouldering
Emissary of fire.

By the wayside, newly woken families stood, confused by the
Spectacle on the hill, hushing their excited children. The men
Followed after, plucking up whatever weapon came to hand,
An improvised army with spear, stave, pick and scythe.
Out of the shadows, a figure darted, grasping at Gwentor's
Harness with crooked fingers, a man with mud-stained robe,
Pale lined face gleaming within the hood. 'My lord, hear me!
Time is short,' he cried, as the five companions surrounded
Him. Edric raised his hand in restraint. 'Put up your swords.
We'll hear him speak.'

'I am Mœlwyn, hermit of the hills, one-time monk at
Haughmond, dweller in the caves of the Stippled Stones.
I bring you a talisman which will hold off this devilry.'
The monk pulled from his robe a circle of burnished
Metal, a buckler, drawing to itself the light of moon and
Stars, gorging and expanding as all eyes gazed upon it.

Edric took the shield, and holding it aloft, urged his
Horse through the parted throng, until he faced the
Tor where the spilled fire crackled and hissed. Gwentor
Tossed her head and neighed, but held firm her ground.
The figures that gathered on the hill, illuminated
By the flames, looked long in disbelief at the bright emblem,
In which worms of dying fire curdled with the gleams
Of the night sky. Then they turned, and were gone
Into the darkness. 'Come monk,' said Edric, 'We will
Seek an explanation of this portent before the moon
Sets.' Dafydd, bending low to clasp the hermit's arm,
Pulled him up into the saddle behind him, and they
All rode back along the silver-ribboned track.

When the horses were fed and stabled, and wine and
Food brought for his avid listeners, Mœlwyn began
His tale: 'For two years I have lived in the caves and
Tunnels under the Stippled Stones, fed by the kindness
Of villagers who leave me offerings from their table.
No doubt you know of me already?' Edric nodded in
Assent. 'In return, I sometimes walk abroad at night,
Blessing the fields and byres. There are many tunnels,
Far more than I can count, mostly airless, clogged with
Earth and stones, waterlogged when the rain seeps in.
They are ancient, hewn by armies in another age, long

Since departed these shores. They built the tunnels to
Search for treasure of a kind: precious metals and gems.
Some they found, but the veins of ore run deep, and
Much lies undiscovered. Often I hear sounds from
The depths, perhaps the running and echoing of
Underground streams, but on occasions there is a
Tapping, a knocking on rock, as if the miners from
Old times are still there, seeking for escape. The
Sounds in the tunnels are deceptive, and could come
Either from below, or from the open air. So I found,
When I traced the noise of tapping and chipping to
The mouth of a tunnel, daylight clear beyond. Men
Were there with picks and torches, wood to shore
The sagging roof. The miners had returned, but not
Ghosts from the past: a work-force sent by Drænog
To prepare his path to the underworld.'

The monk pointed to the shining shield resting against
Edric's knee. 'This I have unearthed in my searches. It
Must be of great antiquity, and may be the object of
Drænog's desire. Certainly, when you held up the shield,
His forces were dismayed, as though you had already found
What they covet.'

Edric pondered awhile. 'The fire on the hill has raised
A superstitious dread that will not easily be quelled.
No doubt Drænog planned to make my countrymen

Shun the Stippled Stones, so he could search the mines
Without let.' 'Send him an offer,' said Dafydd, eyes
Brightened by the red wine. 'Say we will trade the
Shield if his troops disperse.' 'And if we do such trade,'
Sneered Bleddyn, 'how think you he would treat us
Once the bargain closed?'

Godda picked up the shield, and ran her fingers over
Its gleaming surface, and the central boss of dark bronze.
'Mœlwyn has cleaned it well,' she mused, 'but it is small
Protection for a warrior.' 'Not for one who travelled
Light,' said Edric. 'In skilled hands, it would be ample
Defence, whilst the sword weaved. And held in the
Sun's rays it could dazzle advancing troops, and sway
Their minds.' 'See, on the boss!' cried Godda, peering
Close, 'a painted shape: a beast? A bird?' Mœlwyn
Leaned forward. 'As I scraped and polished, the
Picture came to life, out of the deep grime. It is
A bird, a raven I believe.' Edric turned to Ælfric,
Quietly supping his wine. 'Here, my story-teller,
My poet, sit not there dumb: search your store
Of tales, and say if there are any in which the
Raven flies.'

Ælfric coughed to clear his throat, and then began,
His speech quickening as his thoughts gathered.
'The god-warriors of old had raven-messengers,

Scouring the land for sight of enemies. Often
In battle, the birds would fly ahead, circling
Above, swooping upon the advancing foe, and
Mobbing as they would the plundering hawk.'
'And are there any tales of ravens in our Shropshire
Lore?' Ælfric thought hard, and shook his head.
'I know of none. But it may be my Sire, who was
Poet and teller of tales long before me, can
Search his memory.' 'Tomorrow, we seek out
Ælfric the Elder, if the wine has not stopped our
Tongues between times.'

Ælfric's father lived by the riverbank, where he could
Hear the rushing water, and the calls of woodland birds,
For he was blind but relished the sounds around him.
The old tales still flowed in his brain, undimmed by age.
His son questioned him, and the old man ransacked his sheaf
Of recollections. 'There is the story of Cawr,' he said,
After a long pause. 'But Cawr lived in the far west,' argued
His son. 'A giant-killer, and himself a giant amongst men.'
'He came to these parts,' persisted the Elder, 'and died here.'
Ælfric pursed his lips in disagreement. 'No, father,
You are confused. Cawr lived and died in Erin.'
'He crossed the sea and fought the Giant of Yr Wyddfa.
There he lost his two raven-companions, killed by

Sling-shots. Then he heard of the Snow Giant of the Clee,
And came in pursuit.' The father got into his stride,
The story unfolding as he chewed on a piece of meat.
'Cawr approached the Clee, and was attacked by the
Ice-Warriors who guarded the Giant. He fought only
With sword and shield, and the warriors used spear
And sling. His shield, although only small, deflected
The javelins, and chunks of ice thrown from the slings.
He rushed among them, enraged, a mighty man who
Must have seemed a giant to the undersized warriors.
He slew many, and the rest crawled away wounded.
Although Cawr called for the Giant, no one appeared.
He decided the Giant was a fable, or too weak to fight.
So Cawr turned his back on the Clee, and strode away
To the north.'

Here Ælfric the Elder paused, and signalled that ale be
Brought to moisten his tongue. When refreshed, he
Spoke apace. 'He never looked back, only resting when he came
To a place of broken rocks, where the wind moaned, and
Ravens flew in the air like tossed clods of black peat, a reminder
Of his lost companions, and an omen of misadventure to come.
Cawr plunged his sword into the turf, and placed his shield on
The ground beside. The wind whistled fiercely, buffeting Cawr
From behind. He half-turned, catching a movement in the distance
From the corner of his eye. The boulder, travelling through space
So rapidly that its substance was part consumed, struck Cawr in

The back, and knocked him sprawling. He twisted round to look,
And saw far away the luminous white form of the Snow Giant
Of the Clee, lowering his hands after the effort of throwing.
The force of the rock on Cawr's body drove his sword into the
Ground beneath him, piercing him with the hilt, and sent his
Shield spinning away, sliding down the scree, and disappearing
Through a crack. So he died, and the ravens danced in the air above
Him, screeching with harsh voices. The rock under which he
Perished became one with the stone monuments that top the ridge.
As the ages weathered it, his bones crumbled, sinking into the
Earth over which his tombstone rears.'

The listeners were awed. Then Edric asked the question on all
Their lips: 'And where did this happen?' 'Oh, not far away. You
Can see the place from here. The wind still whistles, and the ravens
Still croak over the Stippled Stones.'

Interlude

Riding at leisure, the noble lord Montague sweeps his hand across
The hills and fertile valleys. He is a man of wealth, distinguished
In battle, rewarded by the King for long service. He looks at this
New domain with covetous eyes. Why should the Saxon rabble
Retain such profitable land? Already, he plans the building of his
Castle, assisted by his neighbour lords. There remains the problem
Of the Shropshire earl, a stubborn, coarse man. Without
Declaring open rebellion, Edric has shown an unwillingness to
Comply. He must be humoured, cajoled, given some Norman flattery
That might yet pierce his stiff-necked pride. So Montague takes
The air, with a few well-chosen friends, giving no cause for offence,
Weapons out of sight, admiring the scenery, hoping to encounter
The wayward earl, as if by accident.

Book Three: The Severance

Richness in the pasture-lands, the ripening grain, the easiness
Of riding in the sun. From the high tower on the Myndd, Edric
Saw in his mind's eye the burgeoning defences of wall and
Ditch, the digging-in of armies for a lengthy siege. Though
Threatened, he still felt hale against the rising tide.

He saw the horsemen riding through his fields, clad in festive
Garb, plucking stalks of wheat and laughing loud. They showed
No sword, no mail, no helm, but Edric recognised their kind,
Usurpers in disguise. One of the men looked up, and raised his
Hand, beckoning. The earl approached, Gwentor stepping soft,
And Gethrin, close at heel, growling as he loped. 'All hail!'
The sweet-tongued man declared. 'I trust we do no harm, Lord
Edric, in sampling your land? 'The only harm I fear is fire
And plundering. Ride on, if these are not your aim.' 'I am
The Lord Montague, and seek only your goodwill. Come,
Accompany us awhile, and we can fix our friendship firm.'

Edric set Gwentor at a stroll beside the much-bedecked black
Mount of Montague. He knew the five companions watched
Nearby, carefully hidden, arrows ready aimed. 'How goes
The conquest?' Edric asked, direct and bold. 'Call it not
Conquest,' retorted Montague. 'We come to mould this
Realm into a more-respected shape, where everyone can
Flourish, and benefit from France's rule.' 'Our land has

Ever flourished well,' said Edric, 'when left untouched
By raiders from the sea.' 'We are not raiders, to be likened
To the Danes. Your ancestors too came from the sea,
And brought great benefit.' 'Yet we forged our way of life,
Merging with the islanders already here. You come to
Impose an alien regime.' 'There has been merging, as you
Put it, for many years between the French and Saxon
Folk. Our presence now but puts a crown on gradual
Improvement.'

'And is your pact with Drænog part of this improvement?'
Asked Edric, striking at the man's duplicity. The Norman
Twirled his fingers, as if seeking for a phrase. 'Drænog
Advises us in certain matters; he does not figure in any
Great plan.' 'He has already violated our territory,
Threatened our lives, tried to daunt my people.' Montague
Licked his lips, a dryness overcoming his eloquence.
'There may be factions within his camp that are not wholly
True, lawless men outside of his control.' Edric's derisive
Snort declared this conversation closed. He jerked his
Reins, prepared to ride away. The Norman's gloved hand
Reached out. 'Stay, Lord Edric. I yet have this request.
Come to parley in a neutral spot, discuss the future, share
Your thoughts.' 'Arrange a place, and make conditions
Safe. I will consider it.'

A time was set, at Bromlow mount, a site with clear
View to be had on all sides of the bare, high hill. A
Tent was erected on the spot, where Montague prepared
A feast to be enjoyed by Edric, and Norman guests.
The men of Edric's choice could make patrol around the hill,
To ensure security. They would be asked, in good faith, to
Forswear all weapons whilst the feast progressed.

So Edric went forth, four of his companions by
His side. The folk from miles around gathered at
His gate, to see the lord depart, and some grumbled
That he was yielding to the foe. As the crowd milled,
Three men slipped through into the yard unseen. One
Had the stigma, deftly concealed, of four fingers only
On his gloved right hand.

When the dust of Edric's departure had died down,
Erwine, who remained as guard, climbed the hill that
Overlooked the house, to watch who came and went.
Godda was within, with two servant girls, anxious
For her lord's return. Her mind was troubled, and
Thoughts revolved around the shield that unexpectedly
Had come to light.

Edric came to Bromlow, with no apparent sign of
Lurking troops or spies. They climbed the hill, leaving
The horses at the foot, with Gethrin crouching near

The pile of weapons that the five men shed. The tent
Flap opened on the crest, and Montague emerged, fulsome,
Warm, ushering his guest into the lamp-lit space. Tables
Were laden with surfeit of food and drink.

Godda looked up, her hands about a kitchen task with
Both the servant girls. A shadow fell across the door,
And Shalkin-Leathershanks stood there, face creased
In a grin. 'What domesticity,' he mocked. His two
Accomplices came through into the room, and made
The servants stand against the wall. 'Now, lady, we
Have work to do, whilst we are unobserved. Come,
Leave the table, and the knives laid there, lest you be
Tempted to try further injury. You see, the girls are
Scared. Put not their lives at risk by disobeying me.'
Shalkin held up his glove, five fingers showing, but
The missing thumb replaced by wooden substitute.
He passed his sword from left hand to right, to show
That he had mastered a four-fingered grip. 'We'll
Waste no time. Bring me the shield. Refuse, and
These fine wenches die.'

Godda faced her enemy. 'The shield is hid within a
Cellar, down stone steps beside the house.' 'Lead,'
Said Shalkin, 'and make no false move.' Out into

The yard stepped Godda, walking as if in a trance.
Shalkin followed, sword close at her back. All at
Once, the sound was heard of galloping hooves,
And Oastwald rode in on his mare. He stalled the
Horse, dismounting in great haste, perceiving danger
To his ward. A man ran from the house, and fired
An arrow into Oastwald's chest, then trained another
On Godda, wide-eyed in disbelief. Shalkin walked
Forward, stooped to pluck the axe from Oastwald's belt.
'Woodsman, taste your steel!', he said, striking at
The fallen man. With gush of blood, the head leaped
In the air, and Godda groaned to see her mentor slain.

From his hilltop vantage-ground, Erwine saw Oastwald
Ride in through the gate. What followed he could not
Clearly see, but heard the stricken cry as Oastwald fell.
Running, almost tumbling down the hill, Erwine rushed
To the defence. He saw, as he came sliding to a halt,
Shalkin push Godda down the steps, and Oastwald's
Blood staining the earth. He baffled the arrow that was
Loosed, flinging his body out of range.

Beyond the cellar steps, a tunnel stretched, stone-clad
And damp, lit by a guttering candle in a sconce. Godda
Moved slowly, still appalled by what she had beheld.
She reached the cellar, pulled the door, and creaking
It ajar, turned to Shalkin as he followed close:

'Soon you'll find the shield, behind this wood, and
Drænog will rejoice.' Shalkin seized the sconce, and
Holding it aloft, pushed Godda aside. He slammed the
Door back, eager to cross the threshold of the dark.

He heard a movement, like rustling in the straw from
Rats disturbed. A light sprang up, a bright beam dazzled
Him. The light advanced, a circle, where he saw, distorted
In its depths, his own image, and the sconce he bore.
A shape rushed at him, the lamp was quenched, and
Hard metal struck him in the chest. He fell down to
His knees, heard the door close, bolt shot home.

Godda grasped Mœlwyn by the arm, thankful that her
Words had warned, saw him, even in the dimmest light,
Clutching to his breast the shield that Shalkin had desired.
'Little did you think your new hermitage would be disturbed
So soon. Stay here on guard. I have business above.'

The Daleath ran along the gable of the house, dropped
On the archer at the door. Teeth did their work. Then the
Beast sprang, leaped upon the table, snarling at the
Third man, spitting in his face. The servant women
Backed away, leaving the man to his deserts. The creature

Sat with bristled hair, and as it gazed upon its prey,
The countenance seemed changed from fur to

Some strange plumage, luminous and smooth, the orange
Raptor-eyes plundering its quarry's mind.

Erwine came breathless, stepped over the savaged corpse,
Peered into the room, and saw the third man, crouched
Against the wall, arms covering his face. The servant girls
Sought protection at his side, weeping and shivering.
He smelt the musk still in the air, but saw no other
Living thing. A window in the next room led outside,
And strands of long, brown hair clung to the ledge.

The voice of Godda then was heard, calling from the yard.
She entered, embraced her women both, and spoke with
Great import: 'No time to stay. We take this man, and
Ride for Bromlow mount. Women, prepare good
Oastwald for the final rites.' Erwine obeyed, did not
Doubt Godda's words. He pulled the cowed man to his
Feet, and dragged him out, towards the stables where
The horses champed.

The feast progressed, the guests replete with food and drink.
Lord Edric kept a watchful eye on Montague and his five
French knights, not dressed for war, but soldiers nonetheless
Beneath the lavish gowns.

The sun was bright, and so they took their goblets out upon
The grass, surveying the hills on every side. Edric's companions
Were spaced around the crest, and said nothing when the
Revellers appeared. A thin pall of smoke rose in the air,
From the Stippled Stones, north of the Devil's Throne. The
Noble host drew breath, a gasp of pleasure, as though inspired
By some great thought. 'A looked-for sign?' asked Edric, now
Suspecting Montague's intent. He gazed on entranced, whilst
Edric heard a distant sound, a shrill faint call, and saw Gethrin
Bound towards the nearby slopes. Montague took no note of
Gethrin's course, but Edric watched, and saw the dog climb up
A hill towards figures, visible to him amongst the trees:
Godda, Erwine and a third, bowed down to the ground. Godda
Raised hands that clearly showed there were no chains.

The knights retreated to the tent again, and now
Emerged with swords that had been hid, brandishing them
With mirth. The four companions, startled, knew themselves
Without defence. 'Now, Lord Edric, I have concealed my
Aim,' said Montague, relishing his words. 'The smoke you
See upon the hill, tells me your wife Godda is in bonds.
Sign over to me your lands, or put her life in jeopardy.'
Edric's head sank upon his chest, he groaned in anguish,
And held out his hand as though seeking for aid. 'You see
I have no choice,' the Earl replied. 'My wife is more to me
Than all my lands.'

The four companions cried in protest, not having seen
The hound run or the figures in the trees. 'This parley
Has been ill-conceived, but I will keep my word: my
Lands are yours, Lord Montague, as certainly as Godda
Languishes in chains.' 'Then sign this deed, and you
Are free.' Edric unfurled the scroll, and ran his
Eyes over the elegant script. He saw the proviso, that
Godda would be released unharmed, and brought back
To Lydbury if Edric signed. He raised the nib, dipped
It in ink, and wondered if this would be his final act.
But when the ink was dry, Montague took up the scroll,
Gave Edric leave to go. Carefully, not looking back,
Edric signalled to his men, and walked calmly down the
Hill to where the swords were stacked. 'Unfaithful hound,'
Said Dafydd, blustering, 'abandoning his post.' 'You'll
See,' said Edric quietly, 'how Gethrin has saved our
Lives today, not shirked his task.'

Shalkin lay bound within a cattle stall, glaring with
Wild eyes through the slats. Oastwald had been carried
To his pyre, his axe—cleaned of his blood—laid across
His chest. Long was the mourning as the smoke rolled
Up. 'Let Drænog see another fire, and know that we
Are ready to avenge,' spoke Edric, his voice almost like
A chant. He turned to Shalkin.

'You have violated hearth and home, slaughtered my friend.
No mercy now for such a cur.' 'Hear me,' cried Shalkin.
'Do not lightly spill my blood. Drænog has knowledge of
Your wife: she is not what she seems.' The crimson rose
In Godda's cheeks, her body trembling like a reed.
'What can he know?' asked Edric, thick-tongued with
Rage. 'You add insult to your crimes.' 'You think your
Wife is pure and loyal. But she is as faithless as a
Whore.'

Shalkin spoke no more. Edric strode forward, broke the
Slats, and thrust his sword into the prisoner's throat,
Twisting it until the gurgling blood grew slow. He tore
His cloak, flung his sword aside, and stamped into the
House. His five companions rushed to comfort him.
'Lord, do not believe such lies!' protested Ælfric, as
Edric cursed, and paced the floor. 'What did he mean?
Faithless? She could not be.' Erwine spoke up. 'My Lord,
I have not told you all. When Godda came upon the
Scene of death and treachery, she knew the plan to
Trap you. No one told her. It was as though she read
The mind of him chosen to send the sign. Yet she
Arrived after me. That creature who follows her, I
Smelt its tang. It fled guiltily as soon as I appeared.'

Edric spread wide his arms, despair upon his face.
The four sisters crowded in the door, to see what

Ailed him. He turned to them. 'Ah, daughters! Would
That Oastwald lived, so I could ask him why
He gave her shelter, what the mystery of her origin.
Perhaps you know. Tell me now, that I may crush
These doubts.' The women stood stiff, surveying
Him with baleful eyes. 'You had no need to ask,'
Said Cwen. 'Oastwald would have been as silent
Then as now he lies.'

A hush descended on the room, as though a curtain
Fell, shutting out all sound. The sisters stood
Aside, and Edric walked between them, contrite,
Ready to ask his wife's forgiveness. But Godda was
Not there. The other familiar people crowded
In the yard, but a cold wind blew where once her
Shape had been. High on the fence, the Daleath
Prowled, agile and sure-footed, tail waving in
Dismissal, lost to sight as he leaped into the void.

Interlude

The night closes upon Godda, wandering without knowledge
In a nebulous place. Thoughts tumble, her past coming to
Clothe her again in distant memories, or the unknown future
Rushing to envelop her. She wonders if her origins are true,
Or the fabric of her fancy. Dimly, she recollects the small Welsh
Homestead where her childhood was spent, surrounded by woods,
Deep in a valley overlooked by proud Yr Wyddfa, secret, idyllic.
Her family saga goes back to ancient times, when heroes and savants
Walked the earth. Now she is the last of that lineage, her mother dead
In childbirth, sharing her grave with the newborn infant, her father
Killed by a marauder who found their refuge, and plundered it.
She fled the valley, with Oastwald, her father's steward,
His wife, and four children, close to her in age. They wandered far
To find another haven in the Shropshire woods. For many years
They lived as they had done in Wales, the children—almost
Her sisters—growing into adulthood with her. She holds the
Shield, received from Mœlwyn in his cell, before she took her
Leave of Edric. Also, she keeps her owl-helm, relic of a matriarch
Of old. Regret and sadness fill her mind. The shield holds meaning
That she cannot fully grasp, coming from the depths of her own
History, and leading to an ending that hovers out of reach.

Book Four: Silvaticus

As leaves wilted and browned on the bough, Edric's heart
Shrivelled. His time with Godda seemed like a fair country,
Once his true home, now closed to him. War was certain.
Montague would not stay. The torrent would come to lands
Now valued less than the memory of his wife.

Night drew near. The sisters put food and water in their packs,
Riding out with Godda's horse on rein. Their one request was
That their father's ashes be gathered in a saddle-bag, against
The day they could return them to home-soil. Edric nodded
In assent, broken in spirit. Dafydd came close to ask:
'This man, the third of Shalkin's band, how shall we treat him?'
Edric waved his hand. 'Drag him out, and set him free to run.
But let Gethrin follow on his heels, so that the run be greater
Than any in his life before. Give him Shalkin's glove to take,
Proving to Drænog that more than a thumb has been severed
To requite our loss. '

When Edric's gates had shut, and darkness fallen, the sisters
Found Godda, roaming on the moor, and gave her comfort.
Together they rode for one last time to Wentnor, where the
Lodge was quiet and bare. No music or dancing would grace
These rooms again. The echoes would remain, but no new
Pleasure felt. They gathered what they could, and closed the door.

Wooden towers, straddling their mounds of earth, sprang up
Beyond the Stippled Stones. The soldiers within the baileys
Swarmed, and from these makeshift castles flowed to form
A gradually converging stream. Men from Drænog's camp
Were sentinels, like bee-scouts on the margins of a hive.
The clanking of armour, and stamping of boots grew louder
As the troops advanced, and Edric gathered forces on a
Knoll near More, where he could see the throng surging
Towards him, light glinting on the steel of sword and helm.

Deep in the valley, hidden in the trees, were ancient ruins,
Stone remnants of the military clans who ruled centuries
Ago, and dug the mines. Edric sent men to hide amongst
The shadowed porticos and mazes underground. If
Drænog's scouts approached too close, arms pulled them
Down into the dark recess, where glazed mosaics spurned
The sun.

Edric's force : his men, and troops from earls and allies
In the borderlands, formed a shield-ring on the knoll,
And when the soldiers came in droves, sweating in
Mail, launched javelin and arrow to halt their climb.
With armoured clash, the shields set bodies rolling
Down the hill, where those who hid rushed forth to
Impale the host on sword and spear.

First blood to Edric, and as draggled armies crawled
Back to camps and moated towers, Drænog's troops
Bemoaned their rout. At Shelve that night, the men
Drank deep, to assuage not thirst but misery. The
Women on the fringe of camp, who satisfied the soldiers'
Carnal needs, were welcomed in the tents. One woman
Moved amongst the bevy with different aim, choosing
Her tent with care. The arms she fell into, when the flap
Was raised, were those of Groden, one of Drænog's
Closest aides, privy to many secrets. He sprawled upon
His couch, breath stinking of ale. 'My lovely, you come
In good time,' he said, speech slurred. 'Here—drink.'

He leaned towards her, thrusting a goblet in her hand.
'Who lies in Drænog's bed tonight,' she asked. 'Ha!
No woman—or man! He has cold feelings to all mankind.
Except his beloved Shalkin, who now lies in a bed of earth.'
'And has he never loved a woman?' 'He shuns them all,
And fears only one.'

The man stroked her face, and pulled her close. She
Thought of the time she last lay with a man, but then
The arms were warm, and eyes lit with love. Groden
Wriggled on the couch, his member bulging beneath
His garb. 'And why does he fear this one?' her voice
Enticed. 'Why should you care? Why should anyone
Care about him?' The spite was now apparent in

His tone, his words spilling from his lips like bile.
'I saw a fine woman once, Lord Edric's wife, he who
Slaughtered us today. I saw her wed, secretly spying
On the nuptials, wishing I could share the marriage bed.
Drænog maligned her, called her whore.' He peered
At her through bleary eyes. 'She is not unlike you, but
Certainly not of your kind.' He started to fumble at
Her neck. 'But tell me more of this woman he fears',
She asked, sickened by his touch. He paused, poured
Himself more ale. 'If you have hours to spend, I'll
Tell the tale.'

'Drænog is an ambitious man: he longs to be king over
All Wales, and to this end, he aids the French, hoping
They will give him the rule. But he is also a brigand,
Stealing treasure and precious objects that will decorate
His hall when he is king. He brought us here to this
Dismal place because he'd heard a story about a
Fabled shield lost in the mines. Edric, of course, found
It first, and spoiled his plans.' Here Groden faltered,
As though losing his thread. 'The woman?' prompted
His listener. 'Not a woman—a girl. His band came to
A secluded valley, just the place for treasure to be kept.
He found no treasure, but killed the man who lived there.
A child escaped with servants, the man's daughter. And
Ever since, the child—who will now be grown—has haunted
His dreams, displaying a face of anger like that of a wild

Beast. Here, fill my cup again—my hands are shaky.'
'And where did this happen?' Groden searched his
Addled brain. 'In Wales, near the Yr Wyddfa range.'

The woman had heard enough. She rose to go, amidst
Faint protests from Groden, who straightway fell asleep,
Snored loudly as she left the tent. She picked her way
Towards the gate, unhindered—all the guards were
Soused—and met outside four women, with the
Horses, waiting in the dark. She hailed the others:
'If Edric thinks me whore, it's true in part, though this
Whoring was to glean not gratify.'

Time came when defeat was sure. The Earl gave choices
To his men at arms: stay and fight on without hope, or
Retreat beyond the Welsh frontier. He was to remain,
Living in the wild, a wanderer without roof or bed, except
The rocky dens dug in the hills. His five companions stayed
By his side, resolved to outlast the war, and still be thorns
In the flesh of the invader.

They found the perfect hiding–place, a string of caves cut
Deep within the cliff, sheltered by overhanging roots, and
Near a running stream. The horses could be stabled here
In airy caverns with arching roofs. Edric's men brought

Vital supplies, blankets and cooking pots, fodder for
Their mounts. Also, the saddle-bag that held the ashes
Of Oastwald, reminder of the day of doom to come.
Gethrin fetched game, and added to the provender
From hunting in the woods.

So Wild Edric he became in truth, and many a company
Of troops would find their passage hindered, or supply-
Lines cut. On one such foray, he came close to Drænog's
Camp, still entrenched at Shelve, high stockade fences all
Around. 'I have a mind to see this man whose treachery
Has marred our lives,' said Edric, gazing at the smoke which
Rose from cooking-fires, and guards patrolling at the gates.
'He would be hard to find,' spoke Bleddyn, 'his face is
Known to but a few. He stays within the camp, and sends
His minions to carry out his will.' 'How to beguile him?
There must be a way.' 'My Lord,' said Dafydd, urging his
Horse ahead, 'I'll call him out. He won't resist a meeting
With his bane.' Before any could prevent, Dafydd trotted
Down the slope, and drew near to the camp, crying aloud:
'Beware! Edric is at hand! Sound the alarm!' Confusion
Amongst the guard was followed by the grating of the
Gate, ponderous and stiff as it opened up its jaws. Sparks
Flew within, the soldiers milled, and dimly in the throng
Was seen a hooded figure, walking with wreaths of smoke
About his form, as if he crossed a fiery battlefield.

The horses, fearful of the din, and maddened by the
Sight of Drænog emerging from the haze, tossed and
Stamped, turning the earth beneath them into trampled
Mud. They spun in a circle, hooves boring deep, splattering
Their riders with pellets of turf. The ground split, great
Gashes spread, making the horses lurch as if on a stormy
Sea. The land collapsed with hollow roar, tilting horse
And rider towards the chasm. The steeds fell, swallowed
By the gulf, discarding their riders like baggage, Gwentor
Scrambling clear with straining thews, but wild-eyed,
Snorting in distress.

Dafydd made haste to cross the ground to his fallen
Friends, but arrows sped to halt his flight, brought down
His horse. He quickly rolled clear and staggered to his feet.
Together they struggled up the slope towards the cover of
Trees. Gethrin followed, but Gwentor gave a piercing scream,
Galloping out of sight.

Troops charged for the hill, swearing and hurling spears,
But Edric and the five turned to engage them, forcing
Them back. They almost reached the trees, when more
Troops poured forth, barring the way ahead. The
Pincers closed, men rushing upon them from all points.
Now it was clear the battle was wrested from him,
Edric took his sword, thrust it in its sheath, and whistled
For Gethrin. The dog came at great speed, and to his jaws

Edric committed the blade. Gethrin raced off, knowing
The destined hiding-place, as Edric picked up a fallen weapon
From the field.

The crush of shields and press of bodies compelled them
To kneel, unable to ply their swords. Blades bit in their
Flesh, and rivulets of blood ran down. The killing
Blows were due, when a strong voice declaimed: 'Leave
Them alive! I have a better fate than instant death.'
Drænog, muffled in his cloak, and face concealed, moved
Through the ranks to gloat over the prisoners. He
Signalled to soldiers close at hand, who pulled the men
Upright, and pushed them towards the hill.

Within the grove, and hidden by the trees, an ancient
Quarry mouldered, long deserted by the miners of ancient
Times, the lair of foxes. Deep pits sank down to blackness.
Here Drænog paused, dismissing all but a few loyal men.
He stepped forward to lean over Edric, pulling back his
Hood to show a gaunt, scarred face. 'I see you start in
Fear,' he said, 'but no, it is not Shalkin back from the dead.
But he was close kin to me, my only brother, and you have
Laid him in the grave. You too shall soon be gone to earth.'
He turned to the men beside him, averting his twisted features.
'Throw them in the pit, a long hard drop with bed of
Stone at root, and pile rock on rock, so that their bodies will
Be crushed, but linger on in pain and darkness for what

Will seem an endless, agonizing night.' The soldiers obeyed,
And flung the prisoners down the shaft, listening for
The thud of flesh on rock, and the distant cracking of bones.
Then hauling slabs of stone from the quarry floor, they
Filled the cavity, sealing it like a tomb.

Mœlwyn, having returned to live in his rocky cell, was out
Walking along the ridge of the Stippled Stones, when he
Spied something strange: an animal running across the moor,
Its head seemingly pierced by a sword which protruded on
Either side. He looked more carefully, and saw it was
Gethrin, Edric's hound, carrying the sword in his jaws.
Curiosity made Mœlwyn retrace Gethrin's course, until
He came to the field with its signs of battle. Up the slope,
And into the quarry led the trail of blood and trampled grass.
Mœlwyn gazed long at a pile of stones standing where once
Had been the entrance to a tunnel, sinking deep underground.
It came to him that Edric and his companions must have been
Cast in here, and the entrance blocked. He closed his eyes, and
Searched for a mind's-eye view of the caves under the hills.
How did this tunnel connect, and was there any other way to
Penetrate its gloom?

It took Mœlwyn two days to find a way, doubting all the while
That Edric and his men could have survived their wounds and
Thirst. When he broke through, and tumbled the rocks aside
A hand grasped his, and he cried aloud at what seemed a
Miracle. Edric had fallen, not into a bottomless pit, but walled-up
Cave. Mœlwyn brought water in a flask, and meat, which Edric
Seized, not stopping for speech until each drop and morsel
Was devoured. 'Now follow,' said Mœlwyn, 'the way is clear
Under the Stippled Stones, through hollow halls and narrow
Passages, barely wide enough to crawl, until the light greets us
Again near the green grass of the Myndd. There I will leave you
To your destiny.' Before they set out, Edric returned to his
Companions, and slipped off their finger-rings, one last time
Lamenting the passing of the brave.

He stood again to gulp the full free air, a figure half-naked and
Besmeared with grime. The dusk was gathering as he climbed
The slope, listening for familiar sound. He roamed across the
Moor, stopping to whistle frequently, looking for sight of a
Bounding form. Gethrin came running, like a shadow crossing
The grassland. The dog leaped to greet him, then went speeding
Ahead, with Edric stumbling after.

They came to the high places of the Myndd, Gethrin dropping
To his haunches, tongue lolling. Shapes rose in the distance,
Dim in the half-light: wild hill-ponies, heads bent to graze.
As Edric approached, he saw Gwentor amongst them, and

Whistled again. The horse turned, and tossed her mane.
Edric drew nearer, holding out his arms, calling softly, but
Gwentor held back. Slowly, Edric circled her, seeing the
Harness and saddle still in place. The mare dipped her head,
And snorted deep in her throat, eyes flashing white and wild.
Edric stepped closer, and Gwentor shied, rearing and pawing,
Grinding her teeth, and lunging at the man. Hooves raised
Above his head, she struck him askew, blood running down
His ear. Gethrin growled, and ran to his side, his back providing
A prop to help his master rise.

They parried, Edric moving round, the eyes of horse and
Man locked in the night-long duel. 'Warfare has made you
Mad, my beauty, but I will not let you go.' At last, the neighing
Ceased, and Edric moved to run his hands along the silver
Flank, she fanning him with her breath, and nuzzling the
Wounded brow. He mounted, both standing firm like
One creature conjoined under the starry sky.

Short distance it was to the cave which once had been
Their haven, and where Gethrin had stowed the sword.
Armed, Edric lifted blade to heaven, and vowed one
More assault on Drænog and his host, even if he should
Move alone against them. Gwentor gathered speed.
The sound of hooves followed, and Edric, half-dazed
From loss of blood, thought his companions rode behind.
'Come!' he cried, 'One last hunt.' They were there, it seemed:

Bleddyn and Rywall stirred and valiant, Ælfric stern-jawed,
Erwine laughing at the fray, Dafydd shaking his head
To clear it of the ale, all thundering after Gwentor, racing
Under the moon.

They came to the crest of the Myndd, where Pole Tower
Reared. Edric looked north, and viewed upon the plain huge
Monoliths of stone belching smoke. He knew not if he
Saw the present or the future, blood pounding in his veins.
The horses still followed, and Edric wheeled to face them:
Not his companions, but warriors in helm and armour sat
Astride. 'They have found my lair,' he thought, preparing
To turn at bay. He charged, sword whirling in the air.
They sat undaunted, four with long hair flowing out behind,
One with a helm, owl-beaked, familiar and heartening.
'We ride with you, new companions to replace the five.'
Edric's voice dried; he could not muster belief that Godda
Had spoken, but gratefully accepted the lovely guise.

To Drænog's camp, drear in the dark, they came, the doomsday
Hunt. Unbeknown, Groden had lured most of the troops away,
Leaving their discredited commander with only a skeleton guard.
The gates lay open, as if Drænog expected visitors. Torches
Flared, and the remaining soldiers seemed dispirited, lurking
In shadows as the six rode in. Drænog advanced, casting off
His cloak, clad now like his brother Shalkin in black leather,
His sword clasped in both hands. Edric hastened to meet him,

Countered a stroke, and then fell foul of the hilt rammed
In his face. Godda raised him, her touch like a curative draught.
He stepped aside, granting her primacy: 'You gave the first blow:
To you belongs the last.'

As Drænog saw her in the torch-light, he recognised the
Woman in his dreams. 'As I have haunted you, so too has
Your presence racked my sleep,' she said. 'Shalkin had strong
Resemblance, and so I threw my blade, thinking to end the nightmare.
But you are my father's murderer: you the destroyer of our
Sanctuary.' She moved towards him, sword cast aside, as
Though to embrace her enemy. He saw only her eyes, wide and
All-consuming, as they entered each other's dream.

He travels along the path out of the valley, blood-stained sword
Still in his grip. The leaves rustle, revealing a creature stalking him,
Moving in the branches overhead. He sees only the eyes, orange,
Unblinking, surrounded by lustrous fur. He starts to run, but the
Beast keeps pace above, does not relent. He falls to all fours,
Sword spinning away, an animal fleeing for its life, a small shrinking
Shape, slithering in the leaf-mould, rolling in a ball. His heart-beat stops,
The world and the dream are spent.

Edric shook his head, as though waking from a trance. Drænog
Lay dead before him, body unmarked, with Godda gazing down.
She took his hand, and led him to the sisters gathered at the gate.
Mae held the Shield of Cawr, and Linn the ashes in the saddlebag.
So all along they had known his hiding-place. Godda smiled, guiding
His hand to her belly, where he could feel the strong kicks within.
No words were spoken, except a whispered: 'Come with us'.

The journey back to their homeland lay ahead, finding once more
The secret valley which had brought them joy, laying the remains
Of Oastwald to rest in a hallowed place. Edric had one last task,
Before he followed them on that road: to seek Old Ælfric, if he
Lived (his friends' sole remaining kin), and give him his son's ring.

Godda and the sisters bade farewell, lifting their hands as they
Rode towards the west. Edric was heavy at heart to see them go,
Fearing this one short reunion might be all they had. He found his
Way in the dark, down to the stream which passed Old Ælfric's door.
The man sat on his step, savouring the night air. He knew the
Tread that came towards him, however soft. 'They said you were
Dead, along with my poor boy.' Edric clasped the old man's hand.
'We were all as good as dead. I came back for a little longer on the
Earth. Here, put your son's ring on your own finger.' Ælfric took
The band, and held it for a while, then gave it back. 'Keep it, my lord.
Take all the rings, and part of your companions' spirit goes with you.'

Edric now rose to leave, but the old man held him back. 'You
Have not heard the full tale of Cawr: I thought of more to tell.
Soon my voice will be silent, and all tales lost, so listen well.
In Wales, where Cawr fought the mountain giant, he loved a
Woman, Tylluan by name. She had the shape-shifting gift,
Sometimes an owl, and sometimes a wild creature like a cat,
But with the visage of a bird mixed with beast. A son was born,
And from this child descended the lineage of Cawr, the oldest
And most secret in the land. As centuries passed, men
Thought the line was lost, but Cawr's descendents lived,
Shunning society. The last son was Cigfran, a man of raven hair,
And, some say, able to change into the bird that once served
His noble ancestor. Cigfran was slain by treachery, and the line
Seemed at an end. But there was one more child: his daughter,
And she has disappeared from sight.' 'And was this woman
Too a shape-shifter?' asked Edric, eager to hear. 'Tis like, as all her
Kind inherited the gift.'

Edric departed, deep in thought. And riding Gwentor, with Gethrin
At his side, he passed out of history. Only one can say if he survived
The journey to Godda's secret abode, or perished on the way.
The legend endures that he and his companions still remain
Immured under the Stippled Stones, against the return of war,
And spoilers, like Drænog, who taint the precious earth.

Epilogue: The Tomb

He finds, as if by accident, a secluded house, deep in the forest
Night. The sound of harp music drifts on the air. He leaves his
Horse, and moves within sight of the open window. Five women
Sit within, fine-looking but with the grey of age dusting their hair.
One plucks the strings, to which his ears attune. A youth stands,
Head cocked, absorbing the beautiful melody. The man turns away.
He has heard tales of chance encounters with the folk of faery,
Hidden amongst the hills. He will not outstay his luck. Returning
On the path, he notices a mound with pale glow-worm sheen.
He moves nearer. Steps fall away, leading to an illuminated cavity.
No human should enter a hollow hill, for there they may remain,
Trapped for eternity. But curiosity wins. The steps go deep,
And shadows loom about him, bricks of clay and slabs of stone
Reflect the light. There in the centre, above the level floor, he sees a
Bright object: Mirror? Glass? He peers closely, and finds it is a
Polished shield hung on the wall which radiates both light and warmth.
A tomb to left and right, one sealed and occupied, the other standing
Open, ready for use. He stares into the burnished shield, and sees his
Own reflection: startled pale face and dark-rimmed eyes. Ripples
Pass over his form, and it seems he is being sifted, tried by
Some external force. Then comes the change: a figure rears,
Bearded and hoar, sword held against his chest, a dog stretched
Out across his feet, a horse standing behind, resting its head upon

His neck. It is a kind of sculpture, but more life-like than stone.
The image fades, but then come the voices: telling the tale, as
The harp plays, enlivening the effigy, revealing the man. It is a story
He will be held in trust to scribe. He climbs back up the steps,
And looking back, sees no light on the mound; the stone is sealed.

AFTERWORD

Edric Silvaticus ('the Wild') was a Shropshire landowner at the time of the Norman Conquest, and led an uprising against King William with two Welsh princes, Bleddyn and Rhiwallon. He appears to have eventually capitulated to the invaders and may even have served in William's army. 'Silvatici', so-called by the Normans, were rebels who lived in the 'wild' and harried the enemy in the manner of Hereward the Wake.

The legend of 'Wild Edric', well-known in Shropshire, has two main elements. For his disloyalty in submitting to the Normans, he is said to be imprisoned in the mines under the Stiperstones in Shropshire, to be called upon if England ever faces another invasion, rather like King Arthur in Avalon.

The other main element is the story of how he met and married Godda, a fairy woman, whom he saw dancing with her sisters in a house in a secluded wood. Godda agreed to marry him on condition that he never disparages her fairy heritage. He failed to keep this promise, and Godda disappeared.

I have kept a few of the historical facts, and the chief elements of the legend, but fleshed these out and adapted them into a narrative epic that is almost entirely fictional. Edric in this poem does not surrender to the French. The legend of Cawr, the character of Drænog, and the origin of Godda are all imaginary, and do not appear elsewhere. The Shropshire locations are real.

I am indebted to informative articles on the internet (www.geocities.com/Athens/Aegean/3532/edric2.htm) and the full legend of Edric is to be found in Charlotte Burne's 'Shropshire Folk-Lore' (1883) or Roy Palmer's 'The Folklore of Shropshire' (2004). The sequence of paintings 'Wild Edric' by Rod Shaw has also been a great inspiration (www.bbc.co.uk/wales/northeast/sites/arts/pages/gallery.shtml?9).

Nigel Sustins